Children's Letters to Santa Claus

~ Compiled by ~
Bill Adler

A Birch Lane Press Book
Published by Carol Publishing Group

A Birch Lane Press Book

Published by Carol Publishing Group

Birch Lane Press is a registered trademark of Carol Publishing Group, Inc.

Editorial Offices: 600 Madison Avenue, New York, N.Y. 10022

Sales and Distribution Offices: 120 Enterprise Avenue, Secaucus, N.J. 07094

In Canada: Canadian Manda Group, P.O. Box 920, Station U, Toronto, Ontario M8Z 5P9

Queries regarding rights and permissions should be addressed to Carol Publishing Group,

600 Madison Avenue, New York, N.Y. 10022

Carol Publishing Group books are available at special discounts for bulk purchases,

for sales promotions, fund raising, or educational purposes. Special editions can

be created to specifications. For details, contact Special Sales Department,

Carol Publishing Group, 120 Enterprise Avenue, Secaucus, N.J. 07094

Design by Steven Brower

Manufactured in the United States of America

10 9 8 7 6 5 4 3 2 1

Library of Congress Cataloging-in-Publication Data

Children's letters to Santa Claus / compiled by Bill Adler.

        p. cm.
        "A Birch Lane Press book."
        ISBN 1-55972-196-0
        1. Children's writings
        PN6231.C32A3 1993
        816' .540809282--dc20   93-25377
                            CIP

Illustrations

Santa Claus:

Last Xmas i asked you for a baby brother.

This Xmas i want you to take him back.

Love,
Susan

Dear Santa

Thank you for the nice Robot toy you gave me Last xmas.

This xmas I would Like you to give me the batteries.

Andy

Dear Santa Claus:

I am not going to write to you this Xmas.

When I know what I want I will send you a fax.

Best,

Bruce

Dear Santa

this is the last
year I will write to you,
I think I am getting
too old to believe
in santa claus.

Love

Maggie

Dear Santa Claus:

My mother needs a new Stove. The stove she got dont cook so good

Love
Helen

Dear Santa

I don't need any new toys this Xmas.

all I want is my own credit card.

your fan

Frank

Dear Santa

I said a prayer for you and I will say another prayer if I get the fire truck.

Your friend,

Randy

Dear Mr Claus
I hope you get my letter
This stamp cost me
29 cents and I don't
have any more money.

Your friend,

Jennifer

Dear Santa Claus

   I am writing this letter to you for my cat Barney. Barney has been a good cat all year and I hope you will bring Barney some mice toys

Love

Paula

P.S. Barney would like a rubber mouse.

Dear Santa

I hope you like our Xmas tree.
my mother put the lights on
and my grandma put on the
balls and my father did nothing

Love
Billy

DEAR SANTA

I WOULD LIKE TO
BE A SANTA CLAUS
WHEN I GROW UP
BECAUSE YOU ONLY
HAVE TO WORK ONE
DAY A YEAR.

JONATHAN

Dear Santa Claus

What did you do before you became Santa Claus?

Were you God?

Merry Christmas

Angela

Dear Santa:

You don't have to leave me any toys for Xmas.

Just leave me the money. I'll buy my own stuff.

Murray

Dear Santa

This Xmas I would like a toy that doesn't break when my father plays with it.

Love,

Michael

Dear Santa

We are very poor. If you put a million dollars under the tree we wont be poor anymore

I Love you

Robbie

Dear Santa Claus,

How old are you?
I won't ask you how old
Mrs. Claus is, because you're
not supposed to ask a lady
her age.

Love,
Susie

P.S. I am a lady, and I am 8.

Dear Santa Claus:
I think you should leave a
big Present for my grandma.
She knew you when
you were a kid.

Love

Jordan

Dear Santa

I hope you give all the toys to the poor boys and girls.

You can give me what's left.

Love

Jeanne

Dear Santa

Why do you only leave presents for good boys + girls ?

It isn't fair to the real kids.

Jessie

Dear Santa Claus

I got an A on my report card.

Please remember my A

when you leave the

presents.

I hope I didn't get

the A for nothing.

Your best friend

Amy

Dear Santa Claus

Grandma needs a new hearing aid and grandpa needs a new cane.
They don't need any toys

Merry Xmas to you Santa

Katie

DEAR SANTA CLAUS:
    PLEASE DON'T LEAVE ME
ANY TOYS THAT COST LESS
THAN $10.
    LAST XMAS YOU ONLY
LEFT ME CHEAP TOYS.
              LOVE,
              BRYAN

Dere Santa

I WANT A Baseball bat that can hit home runs.

The bat I got Last year strikes out Too much.

Your FRIEND
WILLY

Dear Santa

Can you get me a trip to the moon on the next space shuttle?

I've never been anywhere except Salt Lake City.

Your fan,
Howard

Dear Santa
Last Christmas you
left me a sled.

This Christmas
please leave
some snow

Your pal,

Jed

48

Dear Santa Claus:

Please wake me when you come to my house.

I'm the one in the bed with the dog.

Your friend,

Johnny

Dear Santa Claus

I didn't leave you any cookies
this Christmas.

You have to go on a diet.

Your pal
Joel

Dear Santa
How many days do you
have to be good?

I have been good
for 2 days and I
will try again on
Monday

I LOVE you

Christina

Dear Santa

I have been a good girl all year except when I forget to be good which is only once in a while so it shouldn't count against me.

Love

maria

Dear Santa Claus:

How much do you make?

Do you make more than the President?

I hope so because you make more people happy than the President.

Jane

president

santa claus!

Dear Santa;

Please bring a Christmas gift for my dog, my cat, my turtle, my goldfish, my rabbit and my frog.

They really have been very good all year.

Your friend,
Allen

Dear Santa Claus,

My name is Robert. I am 6 years old. I want a rifle, a pistol, a machine gun, bullets, a hand grenade, dynamite, and tear gas.

I am planning a surprise for my big brother.

Your friend,

Robert

Dear Santa

I have been a good boy all year and all I want for Christmas is a magic trick that will make my sister disappear.

Love

Andrew